A
World
So
Filled

Poems

Jeff Price

REDHAWK
PUBLICATIONS

ISBN: 978-1-959346-76-0 (Paperback)

Library of Congress Control Number: 2024947088

Any references to historical events, real people, or real places are used fictitious-ly. Names, characters, and places are products of the author's imagination.

Book Interior Design: Harlie Won

Cover Design: Kristy Cannon Key

Printed in the United States of America.

First printing 2024.

Redhawk Publications

The Catawba Valley Community College Press

2550 Hwy 70 SE

Hickory NC 28602

https://redhawkpublications.com

SCAN ME

Praise for *A World So Filled*...

In *A World So Filled*, author Jeff Price invites us into a world of wisdom and wonder. Like Jeff, this collection will educate as to what it means to be of and in Tennessee. It is a world filled with grit, grace, gratitude, and greatness, and one worth revisiting, perhaps on an unseasonably warm winter day on a patio sitting next to a boon companion with a good book and an ice-cold beer.

—Lisa Kamolnick, President, Poetry Society of Tennessee

The world so filled Price describes in this collection not only invites love but demands it and creates it. Sometimes love comes with great color and noise and sometimes it comes on a gray Tennessee day in silence: *A World So Filled* is a testament to the blessing that it is to be gifted with both.

—Brinn Copp, former student and member of the All-Price Classroom

A World So Filled is a warm gaze into a lived-in experience. Novel in its circumstance, yet reachable in its emotion, Coach Price (as I know him) grants the reader a privileged peek into a life that is enviable in its richness. Inspiration, regret, joy, pain, and, most importantly, love are all in attendance in this genuine walk through an authentic existence.

—Chase Diehl, former wrestler and student

Jeff Price's second poetry collection, *A World So Filled* tells the story of a speaker who has listened for the "Damascus Road voice" and writes to share the love story. With this unified group of poems, Price's "words are maps" for his readers to contemplate time and God's mysteries—musings that link like chain mail passed down from one adventurer to another.

—Seth Grindstaff, friend and colleague

Through intimate tales of love, loss, and the everyday struggles and triumphs of teaching, Price invites readers to notice and wonder in *A World So Filled*. From poignant reflections on faith and family to unexpected connections found between White's Lancelot/Gwen and Taylor Swift's *Enchanted*, his words resonate with a heartfelt sincerity that captures the essence of an authentic, real existence. Whether you're savoring a quiet moment with a beloved book or sharing laughter with friends over suds, *A World So Filled*, with its blend of grace and grit, reminds us of the enduring beauty found in human connections and the landscapes we all call home.

—Alex Kinder, friend and colleague

"Methinks, it should have been impossible

Not to love all things in a world so filled"

-Samuel Taylor Coleridge, The Aoelian Harp

Also by Jeff Price

One Steady Glance: Collected Poems

To Julie
Who shows me every day the meaning of sacrament.

To Dewman "Buddy" Doggs
You were my heart hound.
I'll see you when I get there.

Table Of Contents

Prologue-I think I'll Spend my Autumn Chasing Light   13

Filled With Boon Companions and other Loves

Ten   17
Friday in May, New Market, 1993   19
60 Lines for Dewman Doggs   21
Cooper   23
Trickster   24
Like Her Garden   27
The Ragtag Army   28
A More Mundane Fate   30
Armor   32
Work   34
Sacrament   37

Filled with Walks and Porches-A Couple for Each Season

Saints and Poets-15 June 2023   43
Hotshots, Dewman, and Coyote-4 July 2023   48
Playlist-23 May 2023   50
Phoebus Frees the Porch-25 March 2023   52
Watching the Muster-October 2023   54
Autumn Ocean-18 November 2023   55
These Winter Mondays-January 2023   57
Saints and Poets 2-14 March 2024   59

Filled with Art and Inspiration and other Beauty

Kansas   63
On Once Again Looking Into White's Lancelot   65
Wide Awake   66
Wake for the Maestro   68
The Three   70
The Harp They Hear   73
Auden   75
Postcard Poems   77

Leaning Mirror   78
Sandypuppias   79
Marathon Sessions   80
Getting Me to Listen to Taylor Swift   82
Miggy   90
Usually the Wretch   93
A World So Filled   95

Epilogue-Old Guys Being Good at Shit   99

Acknowledgments   101

About the Author   103

Foreword

Regret is so much harder to deal with than failure

Back to this quote a bit later.

When Jeff and his twin sister, Jennifer, were born, I was 14 years old. Five years later, I graduated high school and joined the service. I came home on occasion but not long enough to really get to know them. They were young and preparing to enter the first grade, and I was hanging out with friends.

Mom and Dad kept me updated on their progress, and I remember talking with them briefly on the few occasions I called home (back then, long-distance calls were charged by the minute and could be pretty costly).

The years passed and Jeff finished high school in 1979 after enjoying a successful high school wrestling career (and wrestling was a part of his life for the next several decades). Upon graduation, he was accepted to Carson Newman University, where his wrestling career continued. He graduated from there in 1983 with a degree in religion. His next stop was Southern Seminary in Louisville, KY, in 1983. Two and a half years into his studies, our father died, and Jeff decided to withdraw from the seminary. He stayed in Louisville, beginning his coaching career at Waggener High School. During that time, he also joined the Army Reserve, where he spent ten years as an intelligence analyst for 11th and 20th Special Forces groups. In 1989, he returned to Carson Newman, where he received his teaching certification in English and Psychology.

I believe this decision to teach was the true turning point in Jeff's life and career. He embraced his teaching and coaching with absolute passion. Jeff was called to be a teacher – while similar in some ways to being a minister but with the ability to impact the lives of thousands of young people. Based on his passion for what he does and the love and respect he has for his calling as a teacher, I suspect he just might have positively impacted many more young minds than he ever could have as a minister.

Over the years he taught, he coached wrestling (his first love), baseball, soccer, football, and cross country. He coached several competitive and successful wrestling teams, one finishing in third place in the Tennessee state tournament. He retired from 38 years of coaching in 2022, but he continues to teach AP Literature at Science Hill.

By the way, Jeff loves dogs and microbrews!

So now let's revisit the opening quote: "Regret is so much harder to deal with than failure". How does this relate to Jeff and his life, you ask?

I believe this quote directly relates to the way Jeff has lived his life. No regrets.

Each time he walked onto the wrestling mat, he faced failure, but he did it anyway—without regrets.

When he entered and then left the seminary, he faced the possibility of failure. What next? But he went back to college, earned his teaching credentials, and constructed a long and successful teaching and coaching career. No regrets.

When he taught his first class (imagine the butterflies he might have had walking into the very first class he would teach), he faced the possibility of failure. But then he became an excellent educator and coach and made this his life's work and love. No regrets.

Many of the poems in *One Steady Glance* were written over years, even decades. He was goaded by a former student to collect those poems and get a book published. And then he did it. In so doing, he "put himself out there" for all to see, enjoy, and critique. Again, he risked failure. The book was a great success, and now he has released his second book. No regrets.

Love. Jeff is a dedicated husband to Julie and stepfather to Tyler. His love for them is unconditional. Anytime you fall in love, you face the risk of failure – you give your all to someone, accepting that love can be risky. Jeff and Julie have built a wonderful life together. Again, no regrets.

Love you, brother.
Bill

Prologue-I think I'll Spend my Autumn Chasing Light

I think I'll spend my autumn chasing light,
Get outside somewhere and then look within—
The proper pathway for an old man's might.

The Smokies today pose too far a flight,
And though The Tweetsie Trail is not its twin,
I'll go there to spend autumn chasing light.

The old Ford truck and bluegrass fit just right,
And Dewman Doggs with his excited grin
Show me the pathway to an old man's might.

The changing of the leaves now only slight,
But fairly soon their party will begin.
I think I'll spend my autumn chasing light.

I read Coleridge and Wordsworth at the height,
Because from then to now their words have been
The proper pathway for an old man's might.

So against glum Jeremiads I'll fight
Each moment, each day find a way to win,
Resolve to spend my autumn chasing light,
Follow that pathway to an old man's might.

Filled

With

Boon

Companions

and Other Loves

Ten

"Marryin' her makes up for every dumb thing I ever done"-Sheriff Bell, No Country for Old Men

It was longer than ten years ago
that I got over teenage love poems—
mostly the mawkish babblings
of befuddled teenage girls,
wired on the right side of their brains,
at the mercy of male contemporaries
connected at a lower level.

We still discuss love poetry,
but mostly in the abstract now,
every day digging for the answer—
that much of the verse on the topic is bad
because there is so much of it.

And as I presume to catch a decade
of this best occurrence of my life,
I find originality a chore, opting instead
to purloin the ideas of my betters,
making myself at best a competent fake,
but hoping nonetheless you'll understand.

Because I know that anxious silence
whenever I wait in our empty house,
and know that Nowlan was right—
that love is finding this place
emptier than a stranger ever could
when I come home and there is no one here.

And I believe Auden,
who spoke of one much like you,
with power to tame both real and imaginary monsters,
because the only thought that scares me now
is trying to live life apart from you,
my god child of the moon and the West Wind.

But most of all I feel like Baca,
that God gives his miracles and blessings
to that which rots and is broken and crumbling,
an image of what a hopeless mess I was
before you opened this field that is our life.

So I, like him, am giving you this poem.

And we prove Peart right,
that there is a ghost of a chance
we can find someone to love
and make it last,
for decades, and decades, and decades,
through this life and the next.

Friday in May, New Market, 1993

for Brian, Dave, John, and Ken

I saw it as something like Tortilla Flat,
us a motley collection of bachelors,
Friday, three weeks from summer break.

Decades have muddled my memory,
but I'm sure it was the four of us.
Ken would bring this garlic bread
and John would grill the steaks.
I'm sure Brian and Dave pitched in,
bringing good company if naught else.

All I did was provide the space,
that house that leaned a little right
towards Hinchey Hollow Road,
uprooted roughly from Route 92
when they turned it into a four lane
and carried four or five miles west
into the heart of Rocky Valley,
front door facing a ponied pasture.

Looking at it now it was like us,
all but Ken plucked from other places,
but just as alien to this one as we were,
set down on a strange spot of turf
on which it didn't exactly fit,
the only door in the whole valley
that didn't face the road.

A three-beer Budweiser buzz,
Marty having yet to deliver us
with the wonder that was microbrew,
the blissful scent of searing steak,
a fine, flawless blue spring sky,
Rites of Passage on the Pioneer,
to my thinking a perfect soundtrack,
and a porch that faced only pasture.

All done, we had a good tuck in,
bellies full of bread, beer, and beef,
Last of the Mohicans on the TV.
We took character sheets and dice
and rolled a party only played once,
but I'll never forget my Celtic ranger,
Seamus Mulloy, who soldiered on
in more than one of my stories.

That day is thirty swift years past,
but still, whenever May rolls around
and I see the end of one more string,
every Friday of Maia's welcome month
I turn back to that fine, idyllic day,
the standard for an ideal week's end,
those four friends, still steady and sure,
and wonder if I have three weeks to go.

60 Lines for Dewman Doggs

Morning.
Mid-September Wednesday.
It is early autumn, like me.
Since we'll walk this afternoon,
I ponder leaving you at home.
You might be a pro on the leash,
but it adds another bit of work
to what is, these days, a labor,
so many minutes of slow running,
the Airborne Shuffle in earnest,
but it makes me sad to think you sad,
so we pile in the truck together.

Together.
And it is a good thing too.
Since today my twice scoped knee
and my never quite right back
choose to stage an insurgence,
crafting a perfecta of pain
that adroitly ambushes and bludgeons
my usually strong and youthful will.
But you and I are out here,
along with two of my favorites—
a pristine, starry fall sky,
and a hoodie to cut the chill.

Chilly,
we navigate this briskness.
Still mobile, still purposeful,
loving this aspect of morning
when we seem alone out here,
having the town all to ourselves
like survivors of some kind apocalypse,
and, as on all days, near the end,
you stop, jump, and, paws on my shoulders,
slather four loving licks upon my face,
a gesture of love, or thanks, or something
good. And I agree. This *is* fun.

Not fun.
The hated department meeting.
That most heinous thief of human life.
But I have time to come get you,
anticipation of your courtyard zoomies
certain to be a stream of bright light
in this darkened corner of bureaucracy.
And you do, as usual, deliver,
mauling my malaise with your unabashed joy,
and as one friend spoils you with cookies,
others with belly rubs, I realize
how much I love seeing you get love.

Love.
You are an adept at relaxation,
sunbathing in your favorite spot,
that warm, open space on our front porch,
supervising as I mow the front yard,
exploring the new landscape out back,
or simply crashing wherever you fall,
tangling your cable in five different things,
then lying vigil on the back deck,
I understand what boon companion means,
grateful for how you help me combat time,
loving you for holding me in childhood.

Cooper

At odd times, my dead visit me in dreams,
and uncritically I pass time with them,
not pausing, nor choosing, until waking,
to acknowledge the incongruity,
the strange sense of surreal, skewed existence
that carries itself as insouciantly
as an old, trusted friend through my slumbers
as sure as breathing, or blinking, or thought.

And while grief may, like a shifty, false friend
attempt to ambush me with its despair,
I never fall to its embittered blows,
because some wise, kind friend assured me once
that when we dream of those we truly loved
who've gone ahead of us through that last door
it is not a malign visitation,
rather a message borne to us in grace,
to tell us that their spirits are at peace,
so instead of revisiting my pain
I take kind comfort in our good fortune.

So with the loyalty bred in your kind,
you visited my dreams that very night,
just hours since you took your final breath,
and crossed the bridge into the Summerland.
Standing behind the deck in our backyard,
and with a younger dog's pluck and panache,
you bayed your goodbye, full-throated and true
in your hound's voice, that song distinct to you,
your body hale, robust, and vigorous,
just like you were when you first came to me—
the ravages of age all washed away,
your chestnut spots no longer shot with white,
arthritis gone, eyesight restored, boundless,
loud and long you called out, letting me know
that you'd been welcomed to that paradise,
that it was just as its adherents claimed,
a place pain and suffering held no sway—
that you were at peace, and I should be too.

Trickster

for Merlyn Merle Blackie Lawless

You were brought to me in a shoebox.

And as you ate that first meal in our house,
I remember you as mostly ears,
and almost named you Weehawk,
Bakshi's noble elf warrior,
then decided against it,
thinking it maybe too esoteric,
then little hawk came to mind,
so I settled on Merlin.

And as you became what you were,
I realized you might be better off as Merle,
or maybe Blackie Lawless,
being much more redneck fool
than wizard of great probity,
a little black cat possessed by Coyote,
a merry trickster through and through,
an adept at making mischief.

Fifteen point five years of tales,
stealing bread off of sandwiches,
sampling any drink left unguarded,
sidling up and ramming your head into hands,
purring with perfect joy at the response,
luring us in when we loved you back,
waiting to deliver a playful bite.

But nothing will top the morning,
having returned from a night away,
you met me at the back door,
head covered with I knew not what,
until you led me to the living room
to show me the tub of catnip
you'd liberated from a high shelf,

its explosion on impact
creating a bed of the stuff
that you had luxuriated in
for who knows how long.
What larks.

There are four pictures in my phone,
chronicles of your politic mischief,
one of you caught red handed
with a new bag of cat food,
like the aforementioned catnip,
this time knocked to the kitchen floor
so you could chew a hole in one corner
and eat your fill.

Another was an apparent rescue—
saving me from a baseball that,
like the catnip and cat food,
had found the floor from some high place,
caught by you after a pitched chase,
held secure in your front paws
while your back claws had at it.

My two favorites though
are of you joining me reading,
one perched insouciantly across my chest,
the other peering around the lower corner
of McCarthy's *Outer Dark*,
checking on me to see what's up.

That's why the other night,
when you gave that inkling of the end,
crawling to that place in the closet
that you'd never been to in your life,
I went and found my book
and sat reading in the chair outside,
hoping you'd come bother me,
and when you didn't take the bait
I could see the end of the string.

And yesterday,
your first in the Summerland,
our house empty of your soul,
I waited for that gut punch of grief,
but something else came instead—
what I sensed in the place
was not so much a darkness
as a certain, clear absence of light,
of the warm glow of easy love,
of the laughter your mischief evoked,
and the bittersweet tension between
the grace filled blessing you were
and the too swift passage of time.

Like Her Garden

for Kiki

I am no gardener.

But she is.

Not that I don't love plants,
I just don't fathom their nuances,
the interplay of food and water,
of soil, and sun, and care,
so that instead of Saint Francis,
I'm more like some benign Dexter,
killing what I do indeed love.

She loves her garden like we love our students,
her front yard a horticultural miracle,
a paean to the power of her craft,
tomatoes, serranos, bell peppers
the building blocks of a peerless salsa,
(which I love),
jalapenos that lay the foundation
for professional grade salsa verde,
(which I love more),
waiting with her, like I did with Aunt Lelia,
for ears of corn that aren't quite ready yet.
She loves her garden like we love words,
and Whitman,
and Tolkien,
and Star Wars,
and Marvel,
and Funko Pops,
and her children,
and dogs.

And I love her
and our friendship
like she loves her garden.

The Ragtag Army

for Jai

Right now three things remain: faith, hope, and love. But the greatest of these is love.-I Corinthians 13:13

I watch the feed,

people who love you
bearing their offerings
to your doorstep—
leaving love letters,
flowers and food,
shout outs and songs,
dances,
even a dinosaur.
(Or was it a dragon?)
Everyone in their own idiom,
bearing their good energy
like little precious gems,
tiny pearls with perfect power,
trinkets teeming with God's greatest gift.

I wanted to make my offering,
a tiny piece of *myself*—
So I brought a book
with a trifecta
of what to me
is life saving medicine:

Dogs,
Poems,
Mary Oliver.

Against this coming brawl
with the Red Devil,
we rally to your banner,
all of us right willing
to take your place.
But since we can't,
we come as we are,
our weapons a motley
of whatever strength we can share,
armed with the best we have,

Our songs,
Our words,
Our dances,
Our faith,
Our hope-
but mightier than all those,
Our love.

We are your ragtag army.

A More Mundane Fate

for Scott, Todd, and Scott

The very days are always fuzzy—
those calendar dates of your leaving,
filmy images diffused by time, and grief,
a thing that used to evoke a touch of guilt,
until realization stoically whispered
that you come to mind every day anyway,
so the actual one was more or less nugatory,
as the ache comes in its same abject way,
heedless of any precise time or date—
So why should the exact one be any different?
the same gelid breeze blows perpetual,
grey, tacking toward some dull, malign void,
one day as similar in sadness as another
like a legion of exactly accoutred soldiers,
a sorrow uniform in its burnished sting.
The others are scattered here and there,
brothers both literal and figurative,
who shared the spirit of those heady days—
an "If I could freeze time" team,
so perfect was that season of life,
Some of them still in close reach,
     Some slightly farther out,
      Some beyond sight,

But somewhere on the grid,
their whereabouts perhaps obscure,
though not impossible to find.

Probably you would wonder
at the ease with which one can fail
at being lost or hidden in this world—
most every one of our little band
merely some electronic missive
from another gathering of the clan
if ever the need should arise.

We'd all prefer that you were with us—
Out there in the world somewhere,
                Maybe close,
                        Maybe not,
but near enough that we could find you—
gladly exchanging the bond forged
from the painful hand we were dealt
on the days you were taken from us,
accepting a more mundane fate
if it meant you were still here,
                Out there somewhere,

In some place we could find you.

Armor

"Some say we are responsible for those we love. Others know we are responsible for those who love us." —Nikki Giovanni

Then
It started two decades ago,
when a shy, troubled girl
took my boring yellow school bus
and turned it into a sort of tour bus
for some sixties steeped bards—
Peace signs and sunshine,
starry nights and good energy,
combining to scream loud love
like a bright, benevolent banshee
a talisman that inspired, yet humbled

There had been others before,
mostly diverse works of art.
There was the life sized Spiderman,
the juvenilia of a burgeoning tattoo artist,
an iron man from the hand of
a future graphic designer,
a dwarf on a careening surfboard
fleeing the maw of a hungry serpent,
countless renderings of War Penguins,
an army of my power animal.

That same affection manifested
In so many remarkable ways—
The Dickens tin filled with wisdom,
a pair of grinning, japeless Yoricks,
a veritable collection of ceramics,
Holy grails, fortresses, vases,
even a topper colored War Penguin.
A mug dedicated to Falstaff,
Posters of Dickey and Kerouac,
And a magnificent mob of stuffed creatures.
But it was only seven days ago,
musing on the gifts of this year's kids
that the real epiphany came,

some still, small, Damascus Road voice
there to chide my bald obliviousness,
compounding the great sad inventory
of my teeming trove of unmerited favor,
the stout building stones of legacy,
so many things I never counted on
when I set out on this work God gave me

Now
They show they know me by their offerings.

Two took extreme care of my three small plants,
myself a hopeless duffer at the task.

Another brought a candle for next year,
one with a scent that makes this space unique.

Of course, one brings a book close to her heart
and this time I'll follow in her footsteps.

The rest, seizing on my penchant for battles,
have armed me like some comic, Ill-Made Knight.
A wizard Funko Cartman at my back
a fine, five dollar foam Excalibur
and words, so many, so strong, like the rings
that make a shirt of stoutest Mithril chain,
and as if that kit was insufficient
to guarantee a win in any fight
one supplies me with God's own ordinance—
A dread, ceramic Holy Hand Grenade.

So I stand, attired in this great wonder,
and muse upon what I guess is their love,
pondering their offerings for what they are
to me, the most humbling of sacraments
replete with sublime, unmerited favor,
and love them for their unpretentious grace,
their affection for this old curmudgeon,
cantankerous, but always on their side,
swearing on their gifts to champion them,

To best honor the love they bring to me.

Work-Another for my dad

May 1974

I was twelve
when we walked together to your garage,
the place rife with a man's odd arcana,
old drills and dollies, hammers and hacksaws
paint and pistons, grease guns, bolts and benches—
So much that was a mystery to me,
all tools you wielded with uncanny skill.

That day you chose the old lawn mower,
battered blue body bearing the marks
of years of yeoman's strong, steady service
in the cause of the fine trimmed lawn,
more than just a little rusty in spots,
but its blade sharp and engine finely tuned,
echoing Solo's words about his boat—
That she may not have looked like very much,
but she surely had it where it counted.

Beginning with the gasoline and oil,
you taught the workings of the old machine,
proceeding then to the the choke and throttle,
saving the starter rope for very last,
imparting that staple of mower lore,
to keep my feet clear of the busy blade.
you let me start it up all on my own,
then showed me what to do to shut it down.
My satisfaction was ineffable—
That I'd been let in on this cabala,
this step toward being a grown assed man.

But then the rite of passage took a twist.

You told me to walk to the block's far end,
and knock on every door until I'd found
enough neighbor's yards to have steady work,
and then to cut their grass the best I could.
My first shot at the game was fine I guess,
because I know I was hired at least twice,
four dollars a yard, eight greenbacks a week,
almost more than my young mind could conceive,
my allowance a pittance in compare.

August 1977

Now I'm sixteen.
I come home on a Thursday after school
and you are waiting for me at the door.
You hand me a silly blue clip on tie
and tell me to follow you to the car.
The suspense ended for me soon enough,
as we pulled in the the old A&P,
you walked me straight up to Milo Padgett,
the bossman at this particular store,
introduced me to him, turned and left,
and in five minutes I was at the end
of a conveyor on the checkout line,
learning what in those days was still an art,
how to bag groceries with speed and skill.

June 2023

Six and one have traded places.
It's Father's Day; I muse on the lesson.
The many plows I've set my hands upon.
In a scant few I possess true talent,
in more than those I haven't the least skill,
but I've won so much more than I have lost,
simply because I had a will to work,
to toil, and grind, and never loose that plow.
I'm certain I've lacked expertise at times,
but you never once spoke to me of that.

So I'm convinced you wanted me to see
that work covers a horde of shortcomings—
And I've tried to apply that every day,
and hope that somehow, wherever you are,
you'll see the man that boy has grown into,
and know that when I know that something counts,
no one can ever say they outworked me.

Sacrament

for Julie on our 25th

There are seven of them,
and me, recovering Baptist
turned Episcopalian in absentia
muse upon them quite often,
because they are said to possess grace,
what the old time preachers,
so much more adept at turn of phrase,
called *unmerited favor*,
and God knows all too well,
if I'm to have any chance at all
I need more than the average miscreant.

Most of them I must admit,
religion degree, ordination and all,
are shadowy spiritual abstracts,
concepts I can't confess to comprehend,
but accept as staples of God's mystery,
a thing that drives so many so insane
but never has distressed me in the least.

I remember both my baptisms—
One too young to understand,
the other a fleeced misadventure,
the error of an enfeebled mind,
tricked into trusting too fully
the strong and ugly ego of one
who made self absorbed Narcissus
look like Mother Teresa by compare—
One for a child, the other a fool,
both of whom God is purported
To shepherd with a special care.

I'm not sure about unction,
but we should do it more.
When I'm green around the gills

I think a good anointing would be
a fine thing, for my mind at least.

I love the Eucharist,
especially the Episcopal way,
offered to all who claim belief,
inclusive in a way that to my mind
would be the way Jesus desires,
and while there is no holy light show,
I understand the absolution there
because I need all that I can get.

My confirmation was cool,
the anointing into the fold full of
that presence of God type of peace
I can lay hold of anytime I stop,
and make myself go to the quiet,
because contrary to the outward me,
I like the still, small voice the best.

And reconciliation is easy.
I'm Baptist to the bone on that,
standing with the Apostle Paul,
and Luther and Calvin after,
like them I claim Jesus as High Priest,
so I don't need another human,
no matter how holy, upright or good
to intervene for God on my behalf.

Ordination I get.
Despite the fact that my ceremony
was more a holy dog and pony show
for Reverend Narcissus than for me,
and at the time I had no real notion
of what it meant to have a true calling.
It makes complete sense to me now:
God called me to teach athletes,
certainly to overcome, but much more,
to understand the true lessons of sport.
He called me to make church in a classroom

and to show novices of language
that He inhabits all the written word,
and the amazing love of my students,
their work, their words, their gifts
is sacramental in itself.

The eyes of experience
would lead me to add two or three,
books and poems and music to be sure,
He's shown His love loudly to me in those,
that sense Wordsworth wrote of that disturbs
me with the joy of elevated thoughts,
how His spirit quickens the written word.

I'd definitely add dogs to the list—
The way they teach about what matters,
their ability to live the present moment,
and to love absent of condition or terms.

But if I couldn't fathom any of these,
there would be one thing left on the list
that would make complete sense,
because every time I look at you,
I understand what grace certainly is.

It is a colossal conundrum—
How someone so kind, and gentle,
patient, understanding, and good
loves someone so short on those,
and evidence of God's mystery
how you've put up with me
for a full quarter century now,
proof positive of both your love and His,
so much in you mirrors the divine,
because as Will Campbell said,
We're all bastards but God loves us anyway.

How you love this bastard beats all.

Of all the things I'm thankful for,
all the beautiful joys of this life,
and there has been a treasure trove,
if I was only left with one thing
for which I am ecstatically grateful,
it would be you.

Of all the unmerited favor
I've had the good fortune to get,
and there has been a bounty—
if there was ever one thing
I most certainly don't deserve,
it would be you.

You are grace incarnate.

Filled

With

Walks and Porches

-A Couple for Each Season

Saints and Poets-15 June 2023

"Do any human beings ever realize life while they live it?—every, every minute?

No. Saints and poets maybe...they do some."-Thornton Wilder

I debate.
The book or The Crowes?
Dewman and I have put in
at King's Commons,
taking our first breaths
of this sublime summer day.

I start with the playlist,
looking for some message
to help me with my choice—
I named it *Mashup*
because it's a lotta good
mashed up together.

I hit play,
and I get the guitar notes,
discordant like the bass
that follows close behind,
then a constant cowbell
interspersed with quick licks,
prompting a cheerful change
in how I'm moving my feet,
forsaking the standard stride,
shuffling to that superb beat,
both combining to evoke joy
and a stepping out of the world.

Stone free,
To do what I please
Stone free
To ride the breeze-

And this is perfect,
because Aeolus is on the clock,
throwing 'bout a bonny breeze,
one of Coleridge's desultory ones,
and I let it carry me to freedom,
no buying or spending today,
no trading time for sordid boons,
just the sweet, slow cadence
of a perfect, plodding summer day.

Stevie Ray is next,
Slide Thing driving the world away,
just his guitar and Double Trouble,
and Buddy gets some love
from the bosslady at *Rouge*,
beautiful inside and out,
fetching in her fine summer fit.

Then *High Head Blues*,
the Crowes pushing the theme,

Sometimes I have a ghetto in my mind
Other times sunshine high head fine-

This is one of those other times.

to

A charmed life it is
At least they tell you so
I got a good idea
It ain't like they say is so
And if it is then let me go
Let me go

to

Any day there might be hell to pay

But in other ways
It makes it seem OK
I'll tell you what I mean
It's not a plot nor a scheme
It's just peace in my mind-

And in this exact moment
nothing is closer to the truth.

Big Head Todd leads us on—
I can see the light of peace
Twinklin' on the other shore.

Buddy gets more love,
this time from his friend Kerrie
at The Terrarium Store, cool
both literally and figuratively
with its low light, and mist,
and its panoply of happy plants—

The Crowes' *Descending* is next,
carrying us on up Main Street,
that slow, opening piano riff
keeping the line moving smooth—

No sermons on ascending
No verdict on deceit
No selfish memorandum
No confusion for me
Not for me-

Everything is clear in this instant.

Lora and Brad's people at The Generalist
have left out water for the local pups.
Sadly, the bowl with his logo isn't for sale.

We roll into Little Animals,

the farthest point of our navigation,
because I think their Denim Man
would be a perfect thing at this moment.
Soundgarden is playing in the bar—

But I'm gonna break I'm gonna break my
I'm gonna break my rusty cage and run

Yeah I'm gonna break I'm gonna break my
I'm gonna break my rusty cage and run-

That brilliant bitter is still on tap,
as well as a Depot Street version,
which means I'll be having two.

This is good, as Khruangbin is next,
with *Two Fish and an Elephant,*
my favorite amongst many of theirs
that I swear cast some charm,
some strong, benign enchantment
that compels me to drink beer.
Bound by the desire for remembrance,
the barman lends me paper and pen
so that I can scratch out as much
of these miracle moments as I can,
and as Buddy and I find a table outside,
Stevie's *Little Wing* glides gently on in
just as Jeff Keeling, newsman,
makes his way past our spot
on a quest for caffeine.

We talk Mariners baseball,
and I promise, as I have since 2017,
to get him his Kyle Seager bobblehead.

This defines dog day to me,
because I'm living like Dewman,
no sweating and whining about my lot,
no weeping for my many sins,
nothing but the moment I'm in,
mainlining
        beer
            and music
                and dogs
                    and summer
                        and friends.

And I don't know if I'm a poet or not—
I'm surely by no means a saint,
but in these moments I realize life,
my hands holding fast to its pulse,
the things that make its true blood,
like savoring the moment we're in,
and loving wanting nothing in return.

Hotshots, Dewman, and Coyote-4 July 2023

for the Granite Mountain Hotshots

Having finished the workout
for the nineteen brave hotshots,
the six brutal rounds a study
in sick and sundry ways to suffer,
body still pretty well pissed at me
for what I've just forced it to do,
no longer making unpleasant motion,
and full content to stay that way.

So certainly it is none too pleased
as it grimly discovers I've decided
to go on and walk Dewman Doggs,
and it moves along, but only just,
slowly, stiffly, plodding, griping
at me all the way to the front door,
arguing for short shower and long nap,
then cursing me for not concurring.

Coyote coyly teases us,
waiting like a disciplined sniper,
letting us get to the front porch
before setting loose a torrent
strong enough to stop the show,
and we trudge on back inside,
waiting for another dry stretch.

I have just about enough time
to unhook Dewman's leash
and change clothes, feeling
body's blessing, its right relief
at this finally arrived fit of sanity
when the rain suddenly ceases,
once again inviting its chagrin
as I slip back into into walking kit,
weather the dog's joy explosion,
get him hooked to the leash,
and take to the sidewalk once more.

We are nearly at the halfway point,
just making the turn onto Holston,
the most scenic, fun part of the trip,
my body finally granting forgiveness
moving more or less normally now
when Coyote drops the punch line
he's been holding like some savvy bard
and lets loose a piss pouring rain.

I imagine he hopes I'll be nonplussed,
but just an hour past I've ground out,
slowly, clumsily, and most gracelessly,
one hundred and eighty air squats,
one hundred and fourteen power cleans,
forty-two halting, jumping pullups,
and a mile and a half of running.
Walking though a warm July rain
seems fully facile in comparison.

Dewman, unfazed as can be offered,
lends not one iota of his own urgency,
still stopping, smelling, and peeing,
the occasional stoic shake of his coat
the only sign that anything has changed
in this being outside that he so loves.

And being halfway has its upside.
Instead of some frantic about face,
we simply proceed with the usual route,
arriving home twenty-three minutes later,
completely soaked, both of us cleaner,
reposing in a slow, sanguine headspace
ready for a short shower and a long nap,
having made this morning a paean to motion.

Playlist-23 May 2023

Twenty-third of May.
What remains of my students
leaves Eastcheap one last time,
so summer is more or less here.

All seems to subtly slow,
no more writing to grade,
classroom packed eerily away,
asking me why I'm still here.

It is a good question.
I've rendered to Caesar aplenty.
The therapy dog in the courtyard
pushes me out the door to Dewman.

We take to this Tuesday street,
one of Coleridge's desultory breezes
foiling any mischief Helios might purpose,
and declares this a perfect day.

I have a Miles Cameron book to hear,
and his hero who fights on a Gryphon,
but I still miss Joe Abercrombie,
the sublime duality of Ninefingers.

58 Songs that are Just Cool
is the name of the current playlist.
it shuffles nicely to Kid Gloves
my favorite song by my favorite band.

This keeps The Red Knight on the shelf.
The long, slow cadence of the day
seems to add clarity to the tune
that I never pause or skip anyway.

Another Rush deep track follows,
A fawn eyed girl with sunbrown legs
Dances on the edge of his dream—
Possibly the best lyric ever penned.

Next is a Jackson Browne favorite,
Lawless Avenues, chorus shot through
with unintelligible but sonorous Spanish,
that 1986 concert so much like church.

Browne again with *Late For the Sky*,
its weepy seventies guitar asking
How long have I been sleeping?
How long have I been drifting along through the night?

Then Counting Crows cover *Friend of the Devil*,
not The Dead, but really damned good,
deftly voicing that fine dark comedy
that makes the original the classic it is.

Big Head Todd is next, *Lost Child Astronaut*,
and I realize I'm mangling multiple lyrics,
which means I'm in so deep I'm singing.
which makes me look crazy but I don't care.

Ryan Adams takes us to the house.
When you're young you get sad…
You get sad, then you get high-
I'm neither young nor sad.

The Red Knight has remained on the shelf,
but that is of no consequence to me
since the breeze, the music, and the sun
have raised their anthem to this brilliant day.

So today it's easy to just let go
and toss that best laid plan to the wind,
gladly hand the helm over to the tunes,
and let the playlist shuffle blithely on.

Phoebus Frees the Porch-25 March 2023

Last Saturday it was 46
when Dewman and I
took to the downtown sidewalks,
sunny enough to be sure,
but Boreas seemed to feel
that was a bit too warm,
so he sent sent his breezy minions
like pesky little devils
to scurry capriciously around
and cool things down,
chasing all but the most tenacious
and properly attired types
back to the warmth of home,
hovering slyly about my ears
and neck with an admonition:
"You can stay out here if you want,
But it's gonna cost you,"
leaving me with a chilly slap,
and, respecting the detente
that I observe with winter,
that most capricious, stubborn,
and brutal of seasons,
gladly took myself inside.

A week later it is 73.
Sunny like last Saturday,
and breezy to boot, but today
Zephyros has a different idea,
sending good angels abroad
to subtly soften the sun,
and bearing a different missive
than last week's blackguards:
"You <u>want</u> to come out today
A perfect one to revel in the sun."

So I shake the winter off the porch,
fill Dewman's water dish,
brush the leaves off his bed,
bring him a new rawhide bone,
retrieve my outdoor writing desk
from beneath the back deck,
fire up the big bluetooth speaker,
find a playlist of thinking songs,
get my laptop in proper shade,
and set to work in the open air
to craft this little encomium
to the sublime of the seventy degree day
and the wonder that is spring in Tennessee.

Watching the Muster-October 2023

It always chirps at me,
and today is no different,
that one pervasive voice
urging me to work, or act,
or just bloody do something,
preferably of eternal purpose,
and I don't begrudge it really.
It has my best interests in mind,
entreating me to redeem time,
just hoping I won't squander it,
and today it's pretty precise,
reminding me of tomorrow
and that thing I need to prepare.

But I'm deep in this day,
parked idly on the front porch,
hindered by the heavy peace
inspired by a long walk's end,'
and Dewman crashing at my feet,
and Geralt of Rivia's adventures
and poems about merciful days,
and the bold concert of crickets
which begins earlier every day,
the proud heralds of Autumn's host
announcing the maple's leaves
arriving slowly in twos and threes,
donning their brilliant red surcoats
like Autumn's proud bannermen,
joining orange and yellow legions,
leaden footed but sure to show,
harbingers of a soon to come day
when winter will forbid days of this ilk.

So I make the voice a promise
to be ready for tomorrow by today,
but for now staying in this very spot
teeming with Fall's brisk and gleaming grace.

Autumn Ocean-18 November 2023

Indolence is a savvy, wily one—
Possessed of a consummate charisma,
he never fails to find the proper words,
or shifty means to gain his desired ends.

Like yesterday, with craft and conviction
spinning attractive tales of sweet repose—
one to the occasional-yet just-desert
of sleeping long in the eye of Phoebus,
another to the nap inducing gifts
of a typical Smokies Pancake House,
that vasty breakfast we only have here,
and, laudatory in extreme of these,
He takes me in like some absolute gull,
until I squander most all my hours
in eating, reading, and snoozing away
a day that should have been spent differently.

And today he opens up with the same,
but I'm not down for a second helping,
unwilling to drive out of my mountains
only to realize that I've fallen prey
once again to that insidious thing
that tricks me into accepting far less
than I should be willing to give myself,
or to the ones who share this life with me.
So, with no clear destination in mind,
no real plan or defined trail in our minds,
we saddle up, trusting in good fortune,
and head into the hills in search of life.

Then, true to Wordsworth's superb sentiment—
That nature never fails her true lovers—
we find a trail, obscured by Autumn leaves,
and follow it, until the noise of cars
is lost, and the woods kindly take us in,
enclosing us in all her sublime grace.
the leaves, damp with the kiss of morning rain
fill the air with autumn's hale, heady scent,
and as my lungs imbibe that strong perfume,
my head is cleared of lassitude's canker,
freeing me to think and see as I should,
and live these moments well and properly.

These Winter Mondays

"Hoping to live days of greater happiness, I forget that days of less happiness are passing by."-Elizabeth Bishop

Another January Monday,
kneeling over the weekend
with grey, frigid fingers,
looting the last breath of Sunday
with a stolid but certain unconcern,
twisting those last gasps instead
into whatever cudgel it fancies that day—
last week it was a bitter, biting wind,
today a murky, mirthless fog.

Venturing into this hazy morning dark
makes no significant difference,
since the entire day promises,
although warmer as the sun rises,
the complete absence of light throughout—
an adroit grey smothering him up,
abetted by Hal's base contagious clouds.

Dewman doesn't care one whit,
he's outside and that's all that matters,
chiding me once more with his unsullied joy,
and realizing that yet again he shames me
with his skill at living in the moment
only heighten my irksome, dull malaise.

All too aware of the icy-breathed fiend
who blasts his windy whispers in my ear,
hoping that this exercise will end
in no more than a mawkish Jeremiad
voicing my abhorrence of the season,
my orneriness rouses my desire
to cheat the chilly bastard of a win,
and so I see, regardless of the fact
though this day is a trifecta of gloom—

miserable, cold, and Monday to boot,
We are out here in its garden of grey,
Dewman and me, having our daily walk
as if it were mid May and passing warm,
instead of nestled in the pleasant bliss
of weighted blankets and a one dog night.
So although the victory is purely pyrrhic,
we're still able to claim it as a win
and lift a snarky one fingered salute,
and a promise to make a weekly date
to meet the frozen bugger in the dark
of every Monday from this one till when
my boon companion and I make this trek
with all the joy that comes at winter's death.

Saints and Poets 2-14 March 2024

"Could I revive within me, her symphony and song…"-Samuel Taylor Coleridge

Thursday in March.

Coleridge was right.

You can lose the thread.

Dewman and I set out,
downtown at noon.

I pick the Mashup playlist,
and *Stone Free* comes up first.
Again.

I'm feeling another good one,
like that other Thursday in June
when Hendrix led off with a bomb
that inspired one of those good ones,
one of those spontaneous overflows
Coleridge and Wordsworth talked about,
its skeleton scribbled in the moment
on borrowed paper and pen
over a Denim Man at Little Animals,
a hymn to the untrammeled effusion
of actually living in the moment,
of those all too few instances
where one feels the pulse of the world,
plugged in to the current of real existence.

The reverie meanders on,
probing my imagination
Stevie Ray's *Slide Thing*,
Gary Clark's *3 O'clock Blues*,
and I marvel at the irony
that the blues can make me so happy.
And Big head Todd in *Groove Thing*
musing on the color of the soul.

Then our path crosses Hilary Delgado,
Captain of the All Price Classroom,
we talk…
And I lose the poem.

The time with her is well worth it,
but…

I go straight Coleridge on the porch,
hands avoiding that waiting plow,
read ten or so verses of *Song of Myself*,
then start assembling the new manuscript,
these consummate stall tactics,
as close to being a writer as I can
without actually writing.

The truth of the thing is this—
I'm afraid of what I *won't* find.
But I start this, and muddle along,
groping in the darkness of my head
for the lightswitch I saw plainly at noon,
but all I can manage is this.

This is my damsel with a dulcimer,
my sixteen lines after the rest were lost.

This is my fifty-four lines,
my cut rate *Kubla Khan*,
my paean to damage control.

<u>Filled</u>

<u>With</u>

<u>Art and Inspiration</u>

<u>and</u>

<u>Other Beautiful Things</u>

Kansas

The music plays
And for the moment I feel
That all these days
Are so fulfilling--

Forty-five years ago you arrived,
mere months ahead of Solo and Aragorn,
and took your place in my best, deepest soul—
a burgeoning nerd with a poet's heart,
already not exactly fitting in anywhere,
and being drawn to the different,
the perfect soundtrack
for Tolkien and Moorcock
and working on Zelazny,

like laying both hands on a live wire
surging with beauty and beatitude,
a singular juggernaut of sound and energy,
an almost euphoric sensory overload,
a meteor swarm of fire and light—
meet me where the feeling is high
let the sound surround you
meet me at the top of the sky
where the colors fly around you-

a violin where there should be none,
its strains weaving like some deft, wild bird
over, between, beneath, around
the guitar of Rich Williams,
a prog rock maestro
nonchalantly throwing riffs
like thunderbolts of virtuosity—
Borne on wings of steel
I have so much to feel-
the drums of Phil Ehart,
a deep track of drummers,
not Neil Peart,
but still a peerless adept,
and as Ronnie Platt sang about miracles out of nowhere,
his voice replete with poise and passion—
not Steve Walsh, but close,
I realized I was standing heart deep
in a river of that very thing,
a miracle for certain.

And as I watch you all, all but one,
at least a decade older than myself,
I revel in a certain ecstasy
of nostalgia and beauty,
and hope, as a fellow greybeard,
that I am as good at what I do

as you are at this.

On Once Again Looking Into White's Lancelot

Knowing this book better than any other,
it would be easy to travel somewhere else.
But I've required them to look at it,
and though I'm not exactly asking them
to do something I haven't done myself,
I crack the well worn pages one more time,
because I feel like I owe it to them—
Beginning with the doomed quest for The Grail,
to make one more read through *The Ill-Made Knight*
and gaze again on DuLac's tortured soul.

This time inside his second miracle,
one that I thought I understood full well,
as it has taught me a twofold lesson,
that grace is how the world's real work is done,
and God can work through anyone he wants,
I found something I hadn't seen before,
another lesson in duality,
as Lancelot begins his his entreaty
with the innocence of a little one,
Looked into the East where he thought God lived…
for once removed his focus from himself
bereft of pride, in humility prayed,
I don't want glory but please can you save…
and asked a boon for one besides himself,
heal this knight for the knight's sake, please do…
Then became God's flawed, feeble instrument,
leaning on grace to make Sir Urre whole.

And in his lesson I found grace as well,
unearthing a thing I'd not seen before,
on this ground I've traversed so many times,
and indulging the urge to do what's right,
confirms a truth that comforts an old man—
That new ideas wait for me everywhere,
and some things can't be seen too many times.

Wide Awake

for Chris Cornell and my four favorite misfits

You came back from the fog for me Friday,
your voice again at least as loud as love,
screaming on key, like some heavenly banshee,
underpinned by Commerford's creeping bass,
Wilk's steady drum strokes pumping like some pulse,
Morello's Audioslave harmonics—
Four sonic wheels driving me to new tunes,
four elements of sound forging a blade
beating a swath through the fog of decades,
cutting the clouds of time like Stormbringer,
the press of days dispersed like so much chaff—
Bringing me like some ecstatic comrade
to stand shoulder to shoulder with your ghost.

A song that had escaped my ears till now,
known to others but a new track for me,
a statement on a sleep that you abhorred,
but instead of musing on my present wakefulness,
it took me back to where I used to teach,
site of my personal Superunknown,
a place hellbent on stealing minds and souls.
And though by that time I'd mastered the skill
of paying no attention to its pull,
I knew my days were numbered in its muck,
drowned in its morass of myopia,
where Marlow's flabby and weak-eyed devils
slew difference any time it showed its face.

And only now I see what I was then,
simply by trying to follow my own lights,
perplexed at why so many took offense
like Lourde's little boy walking that garden,
bailing water from that most sunless pool,
my mad search leading me to some young seeds
whose light was too bright for that dark corner,
certainly hoping I could marshall them
through this most absurd season of their lives,

through this tangled, strange forest most expert
at multiplying that absurdity tenfold,
not expecting the fine, innocent light
that they brought to my darkness in that place.

Your ghost, this song,takes me down that highway
to that old classroom in upper pod one
where once again I meet that merry band,

Will, little brother that I never had,
first linked by Drizzt, a right misfit himself.

Kade's little body with its mighty heart,
a boy writer on my same quest for love.

Sarah, the flame haired girl poet whose pen
drew lines with strong fire far beyond her years.

Molzon, who decided to dye his hair,
the first in countless discussions of life,
my first glimpse of the wild mishmash of him
his mix of strong love and stark rage combined.

And while there are so many I could name,
your new song casts these four in unique light.

I will always be wide awake for them.

Wake for the Maestro

"Even as you learn to endure the slaughter McCarthy describes, you become accustomed to the book's high style, again as overtly Shakespearian as it is Faulkne-rian"-Harold Bloom on *Blood Meridian*

Picked *Stella Maris* up last week,
having put it down in January
fifty some odd pages from the end,
resolved to finally finish it up,
but moved on to some other thing,
one in a legion of summer whims
that is quite easily lost in the tide
of early June's promise crammed air.

Today it plays like true design.

It's not like the day Yeats left,
no dead of winter disappearance,
no grey, dark cold one for you.
You picked a perfect Tennessee day,
blue, and breezy, brimming with light
and the siren song of summer.

That sorts better with me at least.

Sixty-eight pages left.

I love the lack of punctuation,
mostly for the simple reason
that it makes my kids crazy,
because it requires harder work,
which is Shakespearean in itself
as it beckons us to lift ourselves,
at odds with the dull mainstream
that would dummy everything down.
Besides, it's a pretty simple task
to distinguish Alicia from Cohen.

and all writers know you weren't wrong.
Quotation marks *are* a waste of time.

Thirty-four pages left.
I'm all set for the rereads,
beginning with John Joel Glanton
and the hulking, horrific Holden.
I thought about scouring Suttree first,
but since it was my gateway drug
to you, greatest of our time,
It might be fitting if it was the last.

Twenty-two pages left.

But now the time is upon me.
Realizing that within this hour
I will have read your final words,
treating this like some grand cliffhanger,
unsure of what I'll find at the end,
knowing that Alicia isn't John Grady,
a kid I know as well as any
I've tried to mentor over the years,

and that Cohen isn't Billy Parham,
trying to the end to save his friend,

And knowing that this world of mine
will forever be a slightly lesser place,
bereft of anymore of your brilliance,
your ability to take words and ideas
and transport us all to a better place,
if only for a moment now and then.

The Three

for Sayer, Bishop, and Joseph

Today you sit,
three newfound friends,
usually so bookish and taciturn
in my Fantasy Lit class,
poring with effusive passion
like mad, merry mages
on the brink of breakthrough,
single mindedly focused
like some rapt, raffish rogues
disarming a deadly trap,
poring over Player's Handbooks,
so consumed with pristine glee
at the concept of characters,
that you forget yourselves
and blow right through the bell.

I must admit some guilt
when I wreck your reverie
to remind you it's reading time.

Still, it makes my morning.

A few days later
I'm streaming a fantasy favorite,
fomenting a foul and frosty mood
as right before the final fight
I have to wake one clodpoll up
just after her best blockhead buddy
has asked to go to the bathroom,
probably to answer a recent text
or rendezvous in some rank restroom
to meet a fellow mooncalf for a chat,
auguring into a negative headspace
spawned by those who don't get it,
when they come to my rescue

like Gwaihir's eagles at Mordor's gate
expressing their vociferous dismay
as Tristan, their favorite, is slain.
Their chagrin soon turns to elation
as Arthur avenges his friend's death.
Again, their passion brings me from the brink.
They are my gods from the machine.

Last week of class.
I again observe their marvelousness
when I take their party to Ravenloft,
each white knuckled roll of the dice
followed by either raw, raucous joy,
the deepest of dour, dreadful despair,
or the long, loud, lovely laughter
born of some silly epic fail moment
(for as my friend Russell contends
that there are no bad rolls, just good stories),
like making the ill-fated mistake
of thinking an intellect devourer
would make a really cute pet.

Finally overjoyed
when one gallant of their number,
the paladin who has been absent
for the last two tempestuous days
miraculously reappears just in time
to bring their wizard from death's door
so she can cast a timely spell
that finally brings down the boss
who on Friday seemed surely to have won.

Days after they've left for good,
I ponder what they've shown me,
these three young, unwitting Arthurs,
that there will be sleepers, and cynics,
and dopamine addicted obliviates,
but there will also be the stalwarts—
possessed of adamantine passion,
who transcend the adolescent tripe
that deceives the self absorbed so,
disabling the traps of high school life,
rejecting the vapid codes of teenagery,
just finding things and people to love,
and grappling them to their souls
with hearty, adamantine hoops.

And while I have a duty to both,
kids like these three keep me sane.

The Harp they Hear

for my 2023 Capstone kids

I leave them alone
with the poem
and the questions.

It almost seems wrong.

I like the skillset,
the things I teach them,
the looking beyond the what
to scrutinize the how
the smaller parts of the whole
the miniscule brush strokes
that combined make a masterpiece,
entreating them to see,
as someone once stated,
that words do not contain meaning,
rather that they create it,
to see the graceful play
of the angels in the details,
the pictures that the words paint,
the higher places they can take them.

Hoping they will trust me
when I tell them one day
they can turn off the filter,
toss away the loaded dice
that they'll use as they gamble
what they've learned for credit,
exchanging their academic lens
for the ability to be quiet
and see into the life of things.

I want them to have, like Coleridge,
moments like the one he draws here,
and that I have chanced upon myself,
that make it impossible not to love all things
in a world filled with whatever it is
that opens before them in that moment,
their own warbling breezes,
mute still air,
sleeping songs.

I want them to muse, like us,
on the instruments nature uses
to steal into their thoughts,
cultivating a quiet pensiveness
to help them hear the universal sound
and their place in its sublime song,
their own intellectual breezes
still small voices
God's whispers.

I want them to look, like me,
at where they inhabit a poem,
hopefully not as I do in this one
seeing the sinful, most miserable
man that I certainly am,
wildered and dark, though loved,
but their own, gentler selves
tastes of grace,
profound joys.

I want them to hear that harp.

Auden

"A professor is someone who talks in someone else's sleep"-W.H. Auden

I have the seed of the thing,
the poem about Breughel, and Icarus,
replete with allusion,
connecting me with two songs
by my favorite boyhood band,
one a kinder retelling of that myth,
the other a pearl from a deep, deep track,
between all the lines
so much that you can find...

That's what I want them to do.

To meet you there,
between the lines,
not my gateway into this love,
(Whitman gets that place)
but certainly my favorite,
being, as you said yourself,
"A person passionately
In love with language,"
since your words illustrate for me
with self-deprecating, stoic grace,
two crucial keys to navigate this life:

Don't take yourself too seriously
And have a sense of humor

But the image refuses
to resolve into that perfect path
that I so love to have
when I sit down with them,
because that's what they deserve,
and I want to be just half as good for them
as your poems have been for me.

So I pour one more beer
and keep mining your words,
looking for that one pearl
that might make them love your stuff
just half as much as I do.

Then when it seems
that a clear path will never appear,
hiding like a mischievous child,
you shout to me
in a voice both clear
and packed full of paradox:

Poetry might be defined
as the clear expression
of mixed emotions.

And I realize then
that we'll have to blaze ourselves,
the three of us,
the path to what we need to find.

Postcard Poems

to my West Ridge postcard poets

Reflecting the season they deftly sketch,
their cards come to me like fine little leaves,
and their words, replete with the deep imprint
of all their sights, and sounds, and sensations,
come near me, filling me full with glad warmth,
their weavings fibers of a stronger thread
forging an iron of shared experience.

They bring light to my day, coaxing that smile,
I feel when I achieve that sense sublime
that Wordsworth saw as the door to true life,
and while I certainly love their workings,
I think another thing pleases me more—
that they have found this gift so early on,
and hope they never lay their weapons down.

I pray that they will always have the fire,
the strength from poetry's pure energy,
that they will always use it to find light,
and hope I honor them with this token,
this halting sonnet to Fall's opulence,
and the fine beauty of their offerings,
and the most excellent splendor of words.

Leaning Mirror

Introspection,

Circumspection,

Reflection,

Always tempt us towards obfuscation.

Like Smithson's mirror,
partially obscured by the dirt
at an angle that muddles true perception,
because the obstruction,
and the misdirection,
and the askew view is what we do.

It takes too much work
to stand the mirror straight,
to sweep away the dull detritus
of the crafty deceits of a long lifetime,
so even if that deep debris should fail,
and the mirror should shatter utterly,
we'll plod straight on without a second thought—
easing into the stark, stoic death
of comfort, whatever lets us alone-
Leave the mirror at its uneasy slant,
hoping that it will shatter into dust
or simply leave us to the way things are.

based on Leaning Mirror by Robert Smithson

Sandypuppias

My stepson, trekking along Paris streets,
saw on a town's sidewalk in lion's pose
a canine formed entirely from sand,
head resting on its paws, guarding a doll,
at perfect rest, but ready to leap up,
showing its sculptor well its posture read,
recalled from some other time of repose,
the maker's hand revealing his heart's love;
and if the dog could speak, I think he'd say:
"My boon companion remembers me here,
Look on his Works, ye lovers, and delight!"
Then lies back down with nothing left to say
and in that city, bustling and bright,
passersby revel in the sight all day.

Marathon Sessions

I was seventeen the first time,
a Sunday to Monday in July
when I stayed up almost till dawn
finishing *The Sword of Shannara.*
The next was seven months later,
too deep into a senior year school night,
to finish *The Once and Future King*—
failing to fathom the sybilline aspect
of that particular escape into pages,
much as I didn't understand the book,
but never forgetting that night,
stoically accepting losing sleep,
wondering what book would be next,
much like what was next for my life—
or how White's opus would become
the cornerstone of my reading life
and the bedrock of my teaching,
a book that certainly chose me.

I've repeated these marathons,
long, deep dives into the sublime—
in my twenties going daylight to dark
finishing *Pet Sematary*, one of few
books that actually scared me.
There were the two-session books,
Passage to Dawn and *Into Thin Air*,
stories that demanded to be finished,
or that grinding, dawn to dusk
four hundred and some page run
through *Gravity's Rainbow*, vowing
not to eat that day until I finished
and had that albatross off my neck,
or reading till daylight to finish
Harry Potter and the Deathly Hallows.

The all nighter is harder these days,
sleep confounding the drive of my youth.
But afternoon to evening still works—
that's when I finished *Kings of the Wyld,*
Bleak House, and The *Passenger,*
or Sapkowski's *The Time of Contempt.*

As readers we relish these runs,
our marathon sessions with words,
speed a secondary consideration,
ticking off pages like mile markers,
routes perfect and picturesque,
replete with the sublime scenery
of adroitly designed landscapes,
seeking the finish line's elation,
and its splendid panoply of prizes,
waiting for the next race to choose me.

Getting Me to Listen to Taylor Swift

to Julie and Molly Wilgus and my 3rd period Taylor Swift fans

I
First,

If Freddie Mercury,
or Ronnie James Dio,
or Stevie Ray Vaughn,
or Mark Heard,
or Neil Peart

returned from the dead for one night only,
I'd probably pony up three figures for a seat.

I'm pretty sure that's the limit.

Love Ryan Adams,
but when the tickets went over a c note
I, and my companions to boot,
concluded that our affection didn't stretch that far.

And I've always needed someone to explain her to me,
so when you know Tyler Childers lyrics at least as well as I do,
and you go to the trouble of making me a playlist of her songs,
and tie them to White's Lancelot and Gwen,
the extreme duality of your musical tastes,
married with your conviction,
warrants at least a cursory perusal.

So I leash up Dewman and we set off
to match your due diligence with my own,
him nose down, focusing hard on his smells,
myself, intent like him,

except on words and sounds,
hoping to find some roadmap in lyrics,
some other doorway to their marvelous minds.

II

She opens with an adolescent anthem,
catchy enough and I see the attraction,
but insufficient to move the needle.

The next one is different though.
Walls of insincerity, shifting eyes and vacancy
Vanished when I saw your face
All I can say is, it was enchanting to meet you-
Casting me back to 1998
when Julie took her seat and smiled at me
and said she'd have whatever I was drinking,
the opening riff for our own first sparkling night-
This is me praying that
This was the very first page
Not where the story line ends
My thoughts will echo your name, until I see you again-
That was me, and her lines bought my ear.

Another song passes by,
one I know and never liked much,
played to death at my old gym,
a staple of Sirius XM The Pulse,
an interestingly ironic name for a station
where most of the songs have no heartbeat.

III

She evokes James Taylor in the next track,
and draws me in with nostalgia,
Mud Slide Slim,
and Sweet Baby James,
and my middle sister,
and my childhood.
and she sings about love.

How it burns,
and breaks,
and ends,
then begins again.

Which it always seems to do.

Begin again.
The good part.
So I listen some more.

Two more tracks,
clearly connected to White's cursed couple,
but otherwise unremarkable.

IV
Close to calling a day on this project,
a big enough bite of the elephant for now,
she catches me again...

We could leave the Christmas lights up 'til January
This is our place, we make the rules, to

We could let our friends crash in the living room
This is our place, we make the call, to

My heart's been borrowed and yours has been blue
All's well that ends well to end up with you
Swear to be overdramatic and true to my lover
And you'll save all your dirtiest jokes for me
And at every table, I'll save you a seat, lover, to

Can I go where you go?
Can we always be this close forever and ever?
And ah, take me out, and take me home
You're my, my, my, my lover.

This one works for sure and buys more time.

V
Then three more
that, I must admit,
fit Lance and Gwen well,
but strike no chord with me,
so I hang it up for the day.

VI
In the next one she likens herself
to a cowboy and a bandit.
John Grady Cole is a cowboy,
Peter Quill and Yondu Ondantu
bandits of a sort.

Not her. Sorry.

Then another Lance/Gwen connection
*"It rains when you're here and it rains when you're gone
'Cause I was there when you said forever and always"*-
This is a piano version, and it's not bad.

And I have a quiet epiphany.

She's better with just one instrument.

VII
Then she starts talking about antiheroes,
and she loses me yet again,
because the first one of those I knew
was Elric of Melnibone,
and that's who I think of,
or Thomas Covenant the Unbeliever,
or Malcolm Reynolds,
or Logen Ninefingers, The Bloody Nine.

And I have to beg pardon.
I don't see any of them
in any guy she'd be involved with

No way they could have the juice.

Well, maybe Travis Kelce.

VIII

The next one isn't bad,
a demi dirge that comes near me,
a study in not being worthy
but giving what you can,
bringing me to Julie-

But I'm a fire and I'll keep your brittle heart warm
If your cascade ocean wave blues come

And
I would die for you
(But not in secret)

And
you got a friend in me

And
I'd
Swing with you for the fences
Sit with you in the trenches
Give you the silence that only comes
When two people understand each other
I'd give you my sunshine
Give you my best-

Stopping there,
lingering in the light,
passing on that final melodrama
without making a big deal of the rain.

IX
The next four have smatches
of Lance and Gwen,
but nothing for me,
so I soldier on, looking
for some other pearl,

And the next two
nail The Ill-Made Knight and his queen,

with

Don't want no other shade of blue
But you
No other sadness in the world would do-
Pretty good shit,
and on point for our Ill-Made Pair,

and

Your string of lights is still bright to me-

It works for them.

X
The next song I like.

It's just her and the guitar,
which is better in my book,

And thankful that it's not me *now*,
but she names myriad locations
that I've visited before,
like

I get drunk, but it's not enough
'Cause the morning comes and you're not my baby

or

I take the long way home
I ask the traffic lights if it'll be alright
They say, "I don't know"-

And some good poetry,
like-

I look through the windows of this love
Even though we boarded them up
Chandelier still flickering here

or

Now I'm searching for signs in a haunted club
Our songs, our films, united, we stand
Our country, guess it was a lawless land
Quiet my fears with the touch of your hand
Paper cut stains from my paper thin plans-

This one works for me.

XI
The next to last on the list
gets Lancelot and Guenever,
but her ventures into invective
leave me a little cold,
Sort of like
cowboys,
bandits,
antiheroes.

XII
The last one is good,
and I'm glad,
just her and the guitar again,
and shot through with Julie,

Drunk on something stronger than the drinks in the bar

and

We were a fresh page on the desk
Filling in the blanks as we go
As if the street lights pointed in an arrowhead
Leading us home

and

And I hope I never lose you, hope it never ends…
That's the kind of heartbreak time could never mend

and

Jacket 'round my shoulders is yours

and

Sacred new beginnings
That became my religion

I like that the end came here.

XIII
So as always in these exercises,
I look for the real lesson, that blessing,
that thing that fills me with that quiet joy
and paints that grin of blessing on my face,
whenever I muse on this sacrament
that comes certainly from my vocation,
but much more in the energy they bring,
so pleased that some of them can see the thread
that transcends time and type to form a link
between Swift's songs and White's star-crossed couple—
but most of all I love what they have found—
Music that ignites passion in their bones,
like Kansas, Mark Heard, and Rush did in mine,
and pray that fire will always be with them.

Miggy

Frequently in life,
but definitely in sport,
we live for the miracle—
And at that you were a master.

Your first hit was a walk-off,
a gangly, raw-boned 20 year old
squaring up an Al Levine heater
to the fattest part of the park
near five hundred feet for the win.
And you were just getting started.

Jump to the '03 Series,
and Rocket, 21 years your senior,
in the last start of his career,
thought he'd show his ass
and welcome you to the big show
with a fastball near your nose.

You just stared back at him,
worked him five more pitches,
and parked a deuces pitch away
four rows into the right field seats
for a two to nothing Marlins lead
on the way to a World Series Ring,
the only one you'd ever get.

As a Motor City Kitty
you worked myriad miracles,
but my favorite was not 300,
which I witnessed in person,
fourteen rows behind home plate,
a bonafide bomb to the camera well,
or the two off the Maestro Rivera,
or the moonshot off Sabathia game four
of the 2012 League series sweep,
and Dan Dickerson's marvelous call—

Fly ball left field…
Watch it fly…
GONE!!!!…

It was none of those.

But against The Tribe,
and that loudmouth Chris Perez,
Omar Infante having knotted the score,
erasing a 10-8 Cleveland lead
with a two run single in the tenth,
then you parking a three one cookie
to the left field seats for the walk off,
Perez trudging in shame to his dugout
while you rounded the bases in triumph
and straight into the mob scene at home.

Today no bang seemed apparent,
just whimpers as Giolito went to ground,
nibbling at the edges so you'd fish
but giving you nothing to hit,
then De Los Santos losing all control,
walking you on four errant tosses,
nothing to remotely offer at,
so wrongly ironic your last at bat
was no plate appearance for stat's sake.

But today the baseball gods were kind,
A.J. granting you one last little shot,
one more chance to man first sack,
their grace manifest on the second pitch
as Steven Kwan ripped a wormburner
to the very spot you were standing on,
and you made the putout on your own,
a three unassisted to close your career.

Today one of my students asked if
I remembered the last time I cried,
and I answered her with the same ease
that you did the hardest thing in sport,
because I cried plenty Sunday
some tears of joy for your wondrous run,
some of thanks that I got to see it all
but mostly from knowing it was over,
that your string was finally played out,
that you, the smiling, jocund warrior,
were hanging your weapon over the mantle.

Usually the Wretch

"We're all bastards but God loves us anyway."-Will Campbell

A friend from way way back,
now a wizened Nazarene preacher,
spoke savvily once of grace,
and its odd, uncanny irony,
and its deep, unfathomed mystery.
He observed that it *is* amazing,
so honey sweet like the hymn intones,
when we are the object of its strains,
but harder to sing so roundly about
when it falls to the wretch we despise.

I guess Campbell had it right.
We're all bastards but God loves us anyway.

My first impulse was to admit
that it wasn't too hard for me,
since I'm usually the wretch,
a stalwart in the host of sinners
that Paul said Jesus came to save.
I'm past White's middle age,
that season when, he contends
one can both love God
and break all His commandments
with both frequency and insouciance.

I guess Campbell had it right.
We're all bastards but God loves us anyway.

Most of my book of the hateful
sing *their* virtue, voices shaming Stentor,
filthy with Pharisaic meanness,
prizing their rightness over love,
taking, in Mark Heard's words,
exclusive pride that they abide
so fantastically far from hell,
experts on who will fast in fire,
though Paul himself called them
noisy gongs and clanging cymbals.

I guess Campbell had it right.
We're all bastards but God loves us anyway.

Others are even more mystifying,
the Tom Colemans of the world,
that racist, redneck cracker
who killed a saint with impunity
and died peacefully decades later.
He escaped justice in this life,
and may in the next as well,
regardless of his hateful deeds,
because if grace is truly amazing,
he gets the same as his victim.

I guess Campbell had it right.
We're all bastards but God loves us anyway.

There is no fathoming this thing,
what the venerable old preachers
gratefully called unmerited favor.
And the lesson comes to me,
to understand how it works for *me*
not how it applies to others,
just be relieved that somehow it does,
find it in the many places it abides,
and let it save the wretch that is me,
thankful for this lovely mystery.

Hopeful as hell Campbell had it right.
We're all bastards but God loves us anyway.

A World So Filled

for Marty Velas, Fanatic Brewing, and the world

Mark Heard was right.

Love is not the only thing.

But it's the best thing.

So let's start there.

God loves us.
I'm a bastard,
but He loves me anyway.

Then there is the love of lovers,
Loved ones,
Friends,
Husbands,
Wives,
Kids.

And a dog's love.
Unsullied,
unconditional,
as close to perfect
as can be offered.

Then there is the love of books.
The sublime of the written word,
to hold them in our hands,
smell an old copy of a great one,
gaze upon the pictures they paint,
the songs they weave
when read aloud,
those tiny tastes of beauty
they unfold before us.

And beer.
It completes the spell
that releases the magic
of any remarkable day,
some "I need to have a beer song,"
Big Head Todd or Khruangbin
laying down the soundtrack,
then gripping the glass,
watching the bubbles rise
in a clear golden Kolsch,
the sweet, earthy fragrance
of a dry hopped pale ale,
the bliss of that first taste
of a mighty, malty maibock,
replete with joy, and promise,
spring's advent and winter's death,
and unalloyed memories

These things make that world,
that Coleridge wrote about,
one so filled
that it is impossible not to love.

Epilogue-
Old
Guys
Being
Good at Shit

Old Guys Being Good at Shit

for Jennifer Smith and Tommy Campbell

I

The concept came upon me unawares,
tied to a stake, my right foot newly reaped
of a brace of its nerves, in retrospect
a thing replete with lovely irony—
beginning a couch bound convalescence
assuaged by fatty fried food and Netflix,
watching Woody Harrelson, one day my senior,
and Kevin Costner, five years older still,
portray a pair of aged Texas Rangers
plying their trade with savvy and aplomb,
bringing Bonnie and Clyde their reckoning,
and as I began that latest instance
of tilting with the ravages of time,
I took a certain comfort in their art,
and reveled in the catharsis that came
from watching old guys being good at shit

II

A few weeks back I stepped into the past
to see my favorite boyhood band at work.
Just one of six fewer in years than me,
four of the others in their seventies,
raging with peerless sentiment and skill,
weaving huge, soaring tapestries of sound,
live wires of beauty and intensity,
unmatched, nonpareil, far from the roll
of even the best these days can offer,
planting my feet in a best of two worlds—
one in my oblivious teenage then,
when energy enough could fill me full,
the other in my slower, sober now,
both possessed of a sweet sublimity.
And once again I gloried in the joy
of watching old guys being good at shit

III

And as I and so many I love best,
cross that bright rubicon of threescore years,
I want to navigate what I have left
in the fine footsteps of Norman Maclean-
choosing to eschew all life's shuffleboards,
armed with whatever wisdom I might own,
resolve to love with ever growing strength,
learn finally to live in the moment,
aware of all the beauty on my path,
follow my passions harder than ever,
find new ones that spur small, shining rebirths,
like Owen Glendower proudly proclaim
I stand not in the roll of common men-
win that name of maestro I so covet,
proud in knowing I too am one of them,
myself an old guy being good at shit.

Acknowledgments

W.H. Auden said "The primary function of poetry, as of all the arts, is to make us more aware of ourselves and the world around us. I do not know if such increased awareness makes us more moral or more efficient. I hope not. I think it makes us more human, and I am quite certain it makes us more difficult to deceive." His statement gets at what I hope I did to at least a certain extent in this collection.

First, I want to thank Julie, because she's supported and counseled me through this and any other endeavor of consequence I've undertaken for the past quarter century. She's always supplied me with confidence and positive energy. Thank you. I love you more than anything.

I want to thank the folks I'm pretty sure read at least some of these poems: Kade Jenkins, Russell Minatel, Kiki Garman-Diamond, Brin Copp, Chase Diehl, Seth Grindstaff, Alex Kinder and Lisa Kamolnick. Your suggestions and encouragement mean more to me that I can articulate.

Thanks to my big brother Bill for reading the manuscript as well and writing my foreword.

Thanks to Jai Gervin for her courage and for doing the cover art and for inspiring one of the poems in this collection. You still owe me a workout.

Thanks to Kristy Cannon Key for her adroit graphic artistry on the cover.

Thanks again to Alex Kinder for helping me with the formatting.

Thanks to Lisa Kamolnick for helping me learn to navigate poetry collectives and societies and how all of this works, and for agreeing to write a blurb for the book.

Thanks to everyone who bought a copy of *One Steady Glance*. Your support motivated me to give this another go, mostly to prove the first book wasn't a fluke.

Again, finally, I want to thank every student and athlete I've had the privilege and honor of attempting to mentor. You inspire me, love me, and keep me young. You are the backbone of my world so filled.

About the Author

Jeff Price is now in his thirty-third year as an English teacher, twenty-four at Science Hill High School in Johnson City, Tennessee. He spent thirty-eight years coaching wrestling on all levels, a career which earned him a spot in the Tennessee Chapter of the National Wrestling Hall of Fame and has included stops in Kentucky, Tennessee, and Virginia. He currently resides in Johnson City with his wife Julie, as well as a pair of cats, Mister and Cleo, and his new boon companion in training, Cash the puppy, yet another rescue dog who is rescuing him.